A
WAITER'S
COMPANION

A Waiter's Companion

Jon Bee

Copyright © 2023 by Jon Bee

ISBN: 978-1-959449-63-8 (Paperback)
978-1-961526-39-6 (E-book/Kindle)
978-1-961526-47-1 (Hardcover)

All rights reserved. No part of this book may be reproduced or transmitted in any form or by any means, electronic or mechanical, including photocopying, recording, or by any information storage and retrieval system, without permission in writing from the copyright owner.

The views expressed in this work are solely those of the author and do not necessarily reflect the views of the publisher, and the publisher disclaims any responsibility for them.

To order additional copies of this book, contact:

Proisle Publishing Services LLC
39-67 58th Street, 1st floor
Woodside, NY 11377, USA
Phone: (+1-646-480-0129)
info@proislepublishing.com

Table of Contents

Foreword 1

Introduction 5

    Chapter 1: What is Hospitality? 11

    Chapter 2: Service 101 17

    Chapter 3: What a Manager Expects from You 33

    Chapter 4: Know your Product 43

    Chapter 5: What We Say and What We Do 51

    Chapter 6: Nonverbal Communication 69

    Chapter 7: The Hygiene Boundary 75

    Chapter 8: Things That Can Go Wrong 81

Conclusion 91

About the Author 93

Foreword

Genuine desire.

Pause for a moment, and reflect on those words. See how they sit with you — how they make you feel. What do you genuinely desire? It's powerful, deeply rooted in who you are — to genuinely desire.

The genuine desire to care for and serve others is the hallmark of great hospitality. This world, which at times can be so divided, could benefit from a little more hospitality among its inhabitants. There are countries which require mandatory enlistment in military service. I wonder what the world would be like if we all had to spend a year in the hospitality industry instead, learning the tactics and strategies to win the war over selfishness and indifference.

This industry is more than about restaurants and hotels. It's about looking after the best interests of others, mostly those of complete strangers who you may never see again. In the grandest sense of the word, hospitality is more than what you do. It's who you are. Great service is more of a lifestyle than a training topic. It requires character and an unbelievable amount of emotional intelligence. It's called the Hospitality Industry, but what businesses in other industries may fail to realize, is that they only exist to serve a human need. Every business is a hospitality business.

> *__A Waiter's Companion__ focuses specifically on restaurant hospitality, from the casual to the upscale. A phrase that comes up a lot, especially with newer restaurants, is the idea of executing "fine dining service in a relaxed atmosphere." Call me a purist, but one cannot cut any corners when it comes to fine dining. It is an art form in and of itself. It wouldn't make sense to say, "I'm creating a ballet, but with a lot less dancing." Though the wording might be off,*

the intent is great — what these restaurants are doing is bringing a better standard of service to more people.

For any restaurant looking to offer quality service without all the fanfare that accompanies fine dining, I'd offer the terms "Refined Dining" and "Organic Hospitality." Organic Hospitality is the idea that great guest service starts with the genuine desire to connect with and care for others. Refined Dining is the delivery of an exceptional guest experience for everyone, every time. This means organizing your approach to service and developing your own standards and philosophies that uniquely express your restaurant. Service doesn't have to mimic a particular style or feel to be great.

In my travels, I have yet to meet a hospitality professional with the talent and magnetic charisma of Jon Bee. Over the course of his career, Jon was worked in nearly every type of restaurant imaginable. Though the restaurant concepts were different, they all were much improved having Jon on their team. He's trained innumerable staffs on the fundamentals of providing excellent service. He's elevated the guest experience at every place he's worked which, in turn, resulted in more business, repeat business, and increased revenue.

On the pages that follow, Jon shares key insights that every waiter should know. This book is written for those just starting their career as well as veteran servers who are looking for some fresh inspiration. It's one of those books that, if you read it at the start of your career then read it again a few years later, it will impact you differently.

This book, and the principles it contains, benefit any type of restaurant or hospitality business. It can serve as a starting point for a training program or as a supplement to an already established one.

This book is ideal for:

- *Waiters looking for a guidebook to jumpstart their career, increase their tips, learn strategies on how to successfully interact with the public, managers, and co-workers.*
- *Restaurant managers/owners looking for a book that will help with team building, improve efficiency, and sales.*
- *Chefs looking for a book that creates unity between the Front of House and Back of House, that extols the virtues of menu knowledge.*
- *Voyeuristic foodies who want to peer behind the curtain to see the details that go into proper food service*
- *Anyone looking for an amusing and informative exploration of what it's like to be a waiter in a restaurant and everything they have to know and care about*

One of the reasons why this book is fun to read is that Jon is an excellent storyteller. You will thoroughly enjoy reading Jon's musings, anecdotes, and advice, which can only come from someone who has worked on the front lines of a restaurant
The hospitality industry can be very demanding. It's good to have a companion showing you the way. So here, without further ado, is <u>A Waiter's Companion</u>.

Evan Faber
Founder, MN8 Hospitality
Evan Faber has worked for over two decades helping businesses, across different industries, enhance their guest and customer experience. He is the Founder and CEO of MN8, a branding and business consultancy based in Boulder, Colorado. Learn more at MN8Group.com/Hospitality.

Introduction

After many years of working in hospitality and in numerous restaurants, I began to take notice of the qualities that distinguish great service from basic service. I learned from the servers I worked with and reflected on my own experience. I paid attention to the difference in qualities like technique, word choice, and table presence, among the more seasoned servers versus the style of those with less experience. Over many dinner shifts, I took notes in my order book, and slowly compiled a substantial collection of valuable information. This book is the product of all those notes, organized here, for the new server stepping into hospitality for the first time. What is it that my younger self would have wanted to hear? Or, more accurately, what suggestions did I need to hear? Most of what I learned, over countless busy nights, had become so second nature to me that I forgot I learned them. Someone new to the industry may be unaware of the breadth of details they must learn in order to provide great service. The dining public has no choice but to tolerate basic and even poor service. But they absolutely notice and return to a restaurant for great service. It's my hope to empower new servers with the information that follows to provide a foundation upon which to build confidence, in their job performance and to instill a desire to do better and be better. You can set yourself apart from the herd by discovering a high-value attitude toward your work performance. By increasing awareness, improving technique, and developing insight, a server can come to understand what great service is and what shortcomings constitute poor service. What follows is the most relevant information towards that end.

Serving food is both an art and a science. It combines the ability to integrate the requirements of the job efficiently along with intuition and one's ability to relate to people. This line of work may or may not be your final career choice. Many take on such jobs while working towards other careers. There are, however, huge benefits to discovering your best self and ability while walking the floors of the restaurants of the world.

When you invest in your skills, you will find yourself working for more lucrative parties and securing the most desired shifts. It is well worth your while to make the effort. Restaurant service is a human exchange that plays an important role in a dining experience and the guest's overall opinion of a restaurant. For each table you wait on, *you are* the restaurant for them that night. Good food can be found in many places. It is far less common to find great service as well.

There is much to learn about human nature and behavior when working in the business of feeding people. But because of the job's transient nature, however, restaurants rarely provide the level of training that would be preferred to fully prepare new staff for service. Therefore, it is left up to the individual to discover the little details that come together to create a pleasant and memorable dining experience for the guest.

Over many years as a hospitality professional, I have taken notice of others with whom I've worked and coupled that with my own experience to distill what separates an average server from a professional waiter. Regardless of the time spent in the business, it is a benefit to you, as well as to your employer, to continually strive for a higher consciousness of hospitality. As servers, we provide a product just as the restaurant does; only, instead of food, we provide our service.

This is our product.

The kitchen staff is afforded many opportunities to learn how to operate in a professional environment at culinary institutes and many such formalized training programs. The front-of-the-house staff has typically only learned the skills of hospitality through experience, with little guidance and practically no insight. This book is designed to fill the gaps and, in some areas, the gaping holes in-service training. I will be intentionally redundant to emphasize valuable information that follows, just as a college professor repeats herself to emphasize the most important information in a lecture. It is the waiter and waitress that have the greatest amount of contact with the guest, and a server can make or break a dining experience.

People judge a restaurant's experience on food, service, and ambiance. Let the kitchen take care of the food and the owner attend to the ambiance. But the service is up to you. Therefore, it stands to reason that being well trained is not simply a matter of learning what to say and do as much as it is about increasing your awareness of the basic hospitality standards. We must strive to discover the proper perspective (I say "we" because I am a server, just like you). As we accumulate experience, we realize the most efficient ways to conduct ourselves, and what to say and what to do becomes second nature. When a server is well trained and fully understands their position within the business, they become a true asset.

Just as there is a myriad of personalities who walk into a restaurant to dine, there are many different personalities that provide the service. There exists a temperament that facilitates success as a server. Those who feel a sense of satisfaction from being of service to others excel in this occupation. This is but one of many characteristics of a successful server. What follows are valuable insights, general guiding principles and specific examples that are not present in most training programs, Despite the fact that most restaurants do not provide sufficient training for new servers, they still desire experienced servers. So it becomes the responsibility of the individual to seek out effective approaches and successful techniques. Historically, the learning process has consisted of observation of others and trial and error. This book is a tool that can help you advance your hospitality awareness and improve your ability to understand your role in the dining experience.

As a new server, it can be difficult to recognize how much you don't know. Learning is an ongoing process, a process without end. Therefore, it is very important to remain teachable, no matter how much experience you may have. There is always something new to learn every shift you work, and the teachable moments will not always announce themselves. Train yourself to recognize and seek them out. Remain open to them.

To the untrained eye, waiting tables may appear to be mundane and effortless. In actuality, appearances are the tip of the iceberg. Many elements are coordinated and managed by a professional server to provide a seamless and relaxed experience for the guest. Excellent service stems from a waiter's fundamental understanding of the responsibilities of the job, the priorities of service, and their concept of hospitality. The job's complexity increases as the number of people you are caring for at one time increases. It is especially during these high-volume times that the professional servers distinguish themselves from those who are untrained and less experienced. A well-trained waiter demonstrates their professionalism and skill during these times while an unfocused, poorly trained server crashes and burns and forgets. Which one do you wish to be?

One does not become polished overnight. It happens over time, the result of an accumulation of knowledge, experience, and a continued willingness to remain open to learning. The information herein is crafted to accelerate that process.

There are many kinds of restaurants, all with different expectations and standards. But, there is a common thread of service quality woven throughout all levels of hospitality, and it is left up to you, the reader, to recognize the aspects of the information that follows, that are relevant and valuable in your work environment.

This resource serves as a companion to accelerate the accumulation of knowledge and to help give more meaning to the learning experience. A waiter must learn how to communicate amongst coworkers to provide appropriate service to the guest. They must also learn how to read the guest so they can determine what type of service they require. For now, think of the experiences you gather as tools in your toolbox. As you begin to gather more tools, you become more capable of handling a wider variety of situations. From long ticket times from the kitchen to challenging guests, the more prepared you are with a course of action and what to say, the more successful you will be. Not only will you become more valuable to your employer, but you will also generate a more significant revenue stream for yourself.

Regardless of your awareness at the moment, there exists a standard of service the dining public has come to expect. The sooner you learn this, the better off you will be. The aim of hospitality is to handle guests in a warm, friendly, and generous way. Your product is your service, and you can choose to invest as much or as little in it as you desire. This book simply lays out the information for you to elevate your awareness of the details of this type of hospitality.

I once worked with an executive chef who told me, "I'd rather have an excellent waiter serve crummy food than a crummy waiter serve excellent food." Despite varying levels of restaurant quality, there are standards and attributes that can be applied universally, from roadside diners to fine dining establishments. It is my hope that this resource will accelerate the learning curve for people new to hospitality. And, for those who have walked the floors for a while, perhaps there is something valuable here for you as well. It is my hope that the training you receive from your restaurant, coupled with the ideas and insights that follow, will put you ahead of the game and shorten the time in which you fully discover the hospitality mentality.

Chapter 1: What is Hospitality?

At one time or another, it is said that roughly half of the population will work in the field of hospitality. Restaurant work is but one area that falls under the umbrella of hospitality. If a person wishes to work in food preparation, then their path will take them to the kitchen, also known as the back of the house (BOH). For those who wish to serve food and work directly with the guests, they will find themselves working in the front of the house (FOH).

The restaurant business is squarely placed upon the altar of hospitality. Simply put, hospitality is the quality or disposition of receiving guests and strangers in a warm, friendly, and generous way. The success of a restaurant depends on its ability to attract the dining public and as a result, there is a standard that has developed that restaurants strive for in order to thrive. Repeat business is the goal, and that happens when a restaurant's staff consistently provides attentive service. It is the responsibility of every front of the house employee, from the hostess to the bartender to the server and the busser to do their part to ensure a guest's needs are addressed. Don't allow a guest to feel ignored. When that happens, it is a failure of the fundamental principle of what we are wanting to accomplish in hospitality. A guest is far more likely to return to a place where they felt seen and heard than a place where they were made to feel they were invisible. People remember the way they felt in a place when deciding where to go for dinner. When a person has a bad service experience in a restaurant and that restaurant is considered once again in the future, they will immediately recall the negative feelings they had the last time they were there, and, most likely go someplace else. On the other hand, when a guest is treated in a warm, friendly and generous way, they will be sure to return.

To understand our job, we must first understand the guest. Although there exists a myriad of personalities among restaurant guests, it is most effective to focus on one type of guest. This is the restaurant critic. This person may be employed by a local newspaper or work for an organization that rates and reports restaurant quality. As a server, if you focus on crafting your service to satisfy the restaurant critic, you will certainly be capable of providing appropriate service to the rest of the dining public.

A critic pays attention to every element of the dining experience—your table presence, steps of service, product knowledge, word selection, eye contact, and timing. These are all important elements to be aware of and improve upon. It is true that the restaurant critic (and those equally significant guests) comprise a small percentage of the dining public. These people, however, tend to have the loudest voice when a dining experience is less than enjoyable. In the age of instant online reviews, we must strive for our best service. Therefore, the up-and-coming waiter must primarily focus on developing their skill based on an understanding of what this particular restaurant guest values. Once you achieve this awareness, it will come naturally to you to care for all types of guests.

Our appreciation for the guest begins the moment they walk in the door. It is important to remember that they chose your restaurant over the others in town. Therefore, the most appropriate greeting is a sincere smile and a welcome. Making the guest feel welcome is the job of the hostess as well as all front of the house staff. We must remind ourselves that it is our job to be gracious and helpful towards every guest. This is the most basic and important guiding principle of the job. We want to create an environment within the restaurant that spreads goodwill in the community. Do your part to make your restaurant a happy and comfortable place to be.

Without the customer, there is no business, period. This concept, in its simplicity, is the foundation of how and why we should care about how we, as servers, behave while on the clock. The restaurant business works when several different elements come together so that the guests leave with a memorable experience and a feeling of satisfaction. This feeling inspires them to tell others of their experience, and it also brings them back through the door down the line. It's that simple.

On the other hand, if any one of the major elements of the experience falls short of satisfactory, then it creates quite another dynamic in the mind of that guest as they leave. Instead of telling three or four others of their enjoyable experience, they may tell ten or more people about the substandard experience at XYZ. Let the kitchen worry about the food and the owner and management worry about the ambiance. The service, however, is up to you.

It is so very important to humbly accept that you have much to learn. The best thing you can do for yourself is to discover, or hold on to, an attitude that enables you to remain teachable. As in life, the job will teach you something new—about something you didn't realize you needed to learn—nearly every shift you work. A know-it-all attitude will only limit you and close you off from growing. And, at the end of the day, it isn't attractive or comfortable for others to work around. A person who remains teachable is humble and modest about their knowledge and experience, and it is usually these people who possess the most useful lessons for those newer to the industry. Learn to recognize those who know what they're doing, and pay attention to everything they do and say regarding guest service and their movement efficiency around the restaurant. This is how I learned and, this book notwithstanding, it is how most people learn.

We must remind ourselves that it is our job to be gracious and helpful. This guiding principle is important to remember, especially when a guest challenges you.

The working environment of a restaurant requires that all of its members maintain effective verbal communication. It may feel at times that you state the obvious and repeat yourself, but from sharing information regarding food items to announcing your physical position behind a coworker, being verbally explicit is an important characteristic of a competent server. We will discuss more on this subject in Chapter 5 (What We Say and What We Do).

When you commit yourself to upholding the standard of hospitality, it comes with pressure to perform that can be quite challenging. The timely delivery of ordered items is the root of this pressure. To be successful, you must learn to operate under this stress. Make no mistake, however, that in the midst of the dinner rush on a busy night, you may find yourself "in the weeds" as we say, consumed with the seven tasks you must do in the next three minutes. As you accumulate experience, you build confidence from knowing what to do, becoming more familiar with food and drink prep times, and a better understanding of guests' expectations. This confidence will manifest in the way you carry yourself. You won't always feel like your head is going to explode, but you will certainly know what that feels like.

When under pressure, identify the next task you must do, then the next, and then the next, but not all of them at once. Train yourself to maintain disciplined thinking patterns. If you allow yourself to become confused and scattered, a breakdown will be inevitable. If a guest has to wait for an item for an uncomfortable period of time, simply say, "Sorry to keep you waiting," or "Thank you for your patience," upon delivery. In most cases, simple acknowledgment is all that's necessary to avoid an issue.

A basic understanding of hospitality should provide you with a proper mindset to approach your work, and your role within the business will become more defined. After laying this groundwork, we can begin to build upward and focus on skills and increasing awareness.

4 Things to Remember:

- The restaurant business is squarely placed upon the altar of hospitality.
- It is our job to be gracious and helpful to all guests.
- Without the customer, there is no business.
- Remain teachable.

Chapter 2: Service 101

It's a nerve-racking experience when you step onto the floor in your first job as a server, with many unknowns and the mystery of experiences yet to happen. There is both an art and a science to this job, and, to become successful, both areas must be developed. The four primary relationships virtually all activity you will engage in as a server are as follows: the relationship with your guest, the relationship with your coworkers, manager relations, and product knowledge. The lion's share of the information that follows address these primary relationships and demonstrates the importance each contributes to your success in your role as a server. Each of the chapters that follow will be anchored in one of these four relationships.

YOUR CUSTOMER

Guest care is a primary responsibility of the server. It is our job to be gracious and helpful towards all guests of the restaurant. The responsibilities towards this end can be broken down into three areas of equal importance: caring for guests' needs, caring for the restaurant itself, and side work, which includes preparation for service and ongoing maintenance of readiness during service. Becoming adept in all of these areas is a priority for a competent server.

Often, a new server can place too much emphasis upon guest interaction at the expense of the other responsibilities. It is important, however, to balance each area of responsibility properly. An example of this is the propensity to stay at a table with a chatty guest for too long. It is part of hospitality to be friendly and engaging, but, along with that comes the development of the skills to break rapport when appropriate. This is a skill set in and of itself. It is a component in the art of conversation to be able to skillfully engage, interact, and end an interaction without awkwardness.

A professional server is aware of the importance of their appearance, so we must see to it that we arrive presentable and ready for service. Our appearance should be clean and professional. Hairstyles should not require maintenance throughout the shift. Wear long hair in a hands-free style out of the face. Not only does this provide a more professional appearance, but it also honors the hygiene boundary between us and the guest that we, as servers, must respect. It is not considered sanitary to touch our hair and then handle items that guests touch. There is more on this subject in chapter 7- The Hygiene Boundary.

Your uniform is to be well presented. Your appearance demonstrates how importantly you perceive yourself as an employee and the respect you have for your employer. It is important to remember that your uniform smell will fade from your awareness but may be noticed by others around you. Therefore, one should not smell of body odor, nor should one bathe in perfume or cologne. Both can be offensive to guests. Save the heavy cologne for your nights out with friends, and strive for a neutral middle ground at work.

No-slip, comfortable shoes are a must, as you will be on your feet for hours and walking on wet floors in the kitchen and dish areas. Shoes are something that mustn't be compromised. The sign of a good shoe is when you can complete an entire shift without thinking of your feet once. Every waiter should have a watch, a lighter, pens, and a corkscrew. Pro tip: Carry a set of reading glasses with you as well as a small flashlight. Guests often forget reading glasses and will be thrilled if you are able to provide them so they can read what your restaurant has to offer. Although we all have flashlights on our phones these days, a handy petite light that can be activated with a simple click is far more convenient. Let guests use it for menu reading in dim light, check signing, searching for dropped items, etc.

Although you may have an excellent memory, it's good practice to write down your food and drink orders. Once you leave the table, it's very common to encounter distractions that can complicate your recall when it's time to place the order. Rarely are guests so impressed as to tip more to a server who can remember an order than to one who writes it down. This advice is given within reason and is more relevant with bigger orders, especially when there are modifications. Because forgetfulness eventually comes for us all, it's a good habit to develop early on.

As you gain more experience interacting with guests, you will begin to settle into your own style of service. Initially, however, learn to pay attention to those around you who have more experience to improve your technique and word choice. There are certain qualities one must develop to find success as a server. Aside from hospitality, friendliness, respect, sincerity, and sociability, there are other attributes one must become aware of and develop. Abilities like dexterity, multitasking, and maintaining focus under pressure are a few examples. But the most important skill, without fail, is the practice of effective communication. More on this comes later. These are all very necessary skills to have in your server's toolbox. They are invaluable characteristics and key to your success.

I'm sure it is quite clear that waiting tables can be a stressful job. It is important however, to present a calm, controlled demeanor in front of guests. You mustn't bring the stress you might be feeling to your table. Remember, your guests are looking to have a pleasant time, and it is your job to do your best to provide that for them. Often, a waiter's facial expression communicates the stress they are feeling. Guests may see that stressed look and feel it, too. All too often, we are so focused on the tasks at hand that we forget about the expressions on our faces. Therefore, a professional server strives not to betray their internal stress by remaining aware of their appearance and adopting a default expression that portrays calm and control. Adopt a pleasant look on your face, as if you're recalling a pleasant experience. Make this your restaurant face. It does make a difference since, at its core, hospitality is a level of consciousness we hold within ourselves. Our behavior on the floor is rooted in this idea and comes through in all of our actions. The way you carry yourself should come to reflect this.

Sense of timing is a key component to ensuring your guests have a smooth and seamless dining experience. Some common issues include food arriving before drinks and the main course arriving before the guests have eaten their appetizers and salads. There exists a template for proper service. Drinks should arrive first, then appetizers and/or salads. Entrees follow, then coffee and dessert. Learn to enter orders so that one course does not crash into the previous one. You direct the action at your table. Learn the pace of the kitchen and how it changes when different people are working back there. Discover what items have long fire times and which ones come up in just a few minutes. The goal is to be in sync with the restaurant and its workers. As the meal winds down, don't begin selling dessert before all main course dishes are cleared. It's inappropriate to rush the last eater by doing so. Timing issues arise when you lose your situational awareness. Make it a point to look over your tables and keep track of where each is at in their dining experience.

Multitasking is an attribute that is core to providing excellent service, especially when you have a full section. This idea is closely related to one's ability to move as efficiently as possible around the restaurant. When you take dirty dishes to the kitchen, bring clean dishes out to the workstation. We call this "full hands in and full hands out." If you are heading into the kitchen with dirty dishes and you pass a coworker with a single plate, save them a trip and take it for them. When you notice the creamer for the coffee is gone in the wait station, look around to see if there is anything else that needs restocking before you go to the walk-in refrigerator in the kitchen. When you have a free hand when passing a table that is ready to be bussed, pick up a dirty glass or two and take it to the kitchen with you. There are countless ways to multitask in this job. Take notice and learn from others around you.

During service, you are the advocate for your customer. It's your job to communicate accurately to the kitchen what they want to eat. Prior to serving the guest, it is your responsibility to ensure the quality of their meal. Avoid placing a cold meal or a substandard portion in front of a guest. If your guests do have an issue, say, for example, a cold meal, remove the offensive item immediately. You want to avoid having them look at something they are unhappy with any longer than necessary. For this reason, in restaurants that employ food runners, it is very important to check on your table within a couple of minutes after the food is delivered. We call this "two bites or two minutes check back." This check back is an important practice every waiter should employ. It's important, however, to be sure that your guests have taken a bite or two before you do so. Sometimes, due to conversation at the table, it may be longer than two minutes before it is appropriate to check back. A check back is the guest's opportunity to inform you of anything with which they are dissatisfied or something else they may need. If a guest does have an issue, be sure to learn how your boss would like for you to handle the situation. Do not offer comps to your customers without knowing restaurant protocol and/or manager's wishes. There is more on customer dissatisfaction resolution later on.

As you deliver each course, it is important to make sure your guests have the silverware they need. It can be easy to overlook a spoon when you serve a cup of coffee, but think about what happens if you forget it. The guest must try to get your attention while the coffee cools, and she is not able to begin enjoying it until she can stir in her cream and sugar. This creates a frustrating situation that should otherwise be a pleasant one. A little detail isn't really a little detail, because something this minor creates a feeling in the guest of not being cared for and reflects poorly on the quality of your service. This small example demonstrates why all the details matter. We strive to create a seamless experience of enjoyment for our guests without creating ill will.

There is no place for pretentiousness on the part of the staff, because without the guest, there is no business. There is a distinction between being proper and being snooty. It is our job to be gracious and helpful. We must remind ourselves of this, even when guests walk in five minutes before closing. Be professional and welcoming, even if you are run down after a long and busy night. Sincerity and eye contact work wonders towards this end. For some, this comes naturally. Others must work to make this part of their demeanor.

At its root, hospitality is a level of consciousness we develop over time with proper insight, and ultimately results in understanding the value of consistent guest treatment. This is an important aspect of excellent service. When guests walk in two minutes before closing time, it can cause frustration. It's important not to forget that these guests chose your restaurant. They deserve the same level of service as those who came in earlier. There will always be situations that will test your hospitality mentality. For you, it will be an ongoing process of fine-tuning your style and attitude towards the guest. After all, this is the job you have chosen, and it should be your primary endeavor to better yourself every shift you work.

YOUR COWORKERS IN THE KITCHEN

A server is the liaison between the guest and the kitchen. During service, communicating the guest's order to the kitchen is top priority. This is usually a simple task unless there are modifications. When there is a miscommunication from the server regarding a guest request that changes a menu item, it usually results in a dish having to be remade. This is wasteful and it is like throwing money in the trash. This includes the consideration of allergies, special requests, and a guest's personal preferences. Modifications are indeed very common, so it is imperative to learn how to communicate these to the kitchen effectively. In most situations, most information can be communicated through the computer. When a restaurant employs an expo—a person who organizes the food in the window and prepares orders for delivery to guests—it is most expedient for all FOH-BOH communication to go through this person. It is more efficient for the line cook to hear one voice instead of many when the kitchen is busy. It may, however, become necessary to ensure your needs verbally with the kitchen. Here is a word of advice here when speaking to a line cook: If it is a busy time, keep your communication concise and relevant. First, get his attention. Then begin to speak. He may not be prepared to listen the moment you approach, so be mindful of this. When the kitchen is busy, all the cook cares about is what he needs to know to complete the order correctly. In other words, there is usually no need to explain extensively why the guest cannot eat cooked tomatoes but can eat raw tomatoes. They don't care about why a mod (modification) is what it is; they just need to know what to leave out or add in to prepare the dish correctly. Some kitchens grumble about such modifications, but remember, you are the advocate for your customer and it is important to learn to work with the kitchen when communicating guest wishes. Sometimes a guest's request may compromise the integrity of a dish. This means that the quality of the dish becomes substandard if a certain ingredient is removed or added. A chef may be reluctant to send out a dish like that. In this case, it may be best to ask the guest to make another selection.

A waiter should consider himself on the same team as the guest. This will put you in the right mindset to provide good service and a pleasant dining experience. In other words, if you are not happy with the quality of a dish, it is your responsibility to speak up and share your concerns. Sometimes it is uncomfortable to voice your concerns to the line cooks, especially when the kitchen is busy, but remember that each guest experience can positively or negatively affect the reputation of your restaurant. Therefore, you must do your part to ensure a pleasant experience.

The communication component includes learning what the kitchen is offering that is not listed on the menu. These are called specials. You'll want to gather this information pre shift. Guests come to expect verbal explanations of some items. This includes the soup of the day and special entrees. If there is nothing offered other than menu items, it is a nice touch to simply say, "Everything we are offering today is listed on the menu." This is a discreet way to say, "We don't have any specials."

Along with knowing what is available from the kitchen, it is also essential to know what is not available. When something, listed on the menu, is out of stock, we refer to the item as being "86'd." This is restaurant-speak for "we are out of…" This is important information to know pre-shift so you can manage your tables professionally. Be sure to check on 86'd items from the kitchen and the bar. If a guest orders an item that is not available and you were not aware of it at the moment, return to the guest with a comparable suggestion and/or a menu so they may make another selection.

There is an interesting dynamic to your job performance: You get an A if you complete a shift flawlessly. If you make one mistake, however, your grade drops down to a C-. We must think of the kitchen as a well-oiled machine. When you enter an order wrong and throw a wrench in it, the works get jammed up. The kitchen staff gets knocked out of their zone and the productive flow is disrupted. That said, we all make mistakes, and they are expected. It's not the end of the world when you screw up, but strive to make as few mistakes as possible. It is advisable to accept responsibility when you do mess up by simply saying, "That was my mistake," or "Sorry, fellas, my bad." Acknowledgments like these go a long way when making an effort to establish respectful relationships. Experienced servers still make mistakes, but they're fewer and far between, and they are more skilled in handling them appropriately.

The relationship you create with the kitchen is key to providing good care for your guest. From product knowledge to expedited issue resolution, there is much to gain by creating a respectful relationship with the BOH. There are also ways to lose the respect of the kitchen. Subpar food knowledge and taking food to eat without asking will certainly lead to this end. The kitchen will always have food out, and it can be quite tempting to eat. It is, however, disrespectful to take without asking. It is very helpful to accumulate food experience in order to become more adept at fielding guests' questions accurately, but do so correctly and respectfully. As a member of the front of the house, it's important to be respectful of what the chef and his employees have created. Not only is it the right thing to do, but it will also benefit you, especially when you find yourself in need of something you forgot to order in the middle of busy service. During service, your primary relationship is with your customer. Maintaining a good relationship with the BOH is a means to that end.

FRONT OF THE HOUSE

It is virtually impossible to provide complete care for your guest without the assistance of your fellow FOH coworkers. Most every restaurant professes the notion of teamwork. When restaurants pool tips, working together is expected, but even in restaurants where each server works for their own money, the teamwork model is usually encouraged and most times, required. When you have downtime, make yourself available to assist others. If you're waiting for drinks from the bar, help bus a table. When your section has one table and your neighbor has four tables, help out by setting up coffee service. The overall idea is to provide good customer service to all guests, even if they are not in your section. When guests feel well cared for, they will return in the future. That benefits you. When your manager sees that you are aware of that dynamic, you will be held in a higher regard than others who miss the importance of this guiding principle. As you make the effort to help others when they need it, it will surely be returned to you when you are in need. This is the Golden Rule—treat others the way you want to be treated—age old wisdom in action.

Success is the result of preparation. Before beginning service, servers put everything in place that they will need to provide excellent service. When they do not complete these tasks beforehand, it becomes glaringly obvious during service when, for example, coffee creamer was not properly stocked, and you must go to the walk-in refrigerator to get it.

Seconds count when you are busy. Be sure to do your part to prepare for service and learn what chores to perform during service to maintain the proper level of readiness. These tasks are your running side work done for the benefit of every member of the FOH. Moreover, when you fulfill your responsibilities in preparation and maintenance, your coworkers will appreciate your efforts.

Servers are also the caretakers of the FOH. It is our job to clean the dining room and do our best to prevent a guest from discovering evidence of the previous patron. Greasy saltshakers, crumbs on the table or chairs, and dirty silverware are all indications of substandard restaurant care. Attention to detail is what sets a professional waiter apart from the vast sea of food servers. It manifests itself in a waiter's sense of cleanliness, the anticipation of guest needs, a determination of what style of service a guest desires, and your word choice. As you fine tune your awareness and technique, you will begin to notice the benefits of your efforts among your guests and your manager alike.

As the night winds down and support staff, like hostesses and server assistants, get cut, be aware of how your responsibilities change. It may become necessary to take on the role of host and keep an eye on the door for late-arriving guests. When server assistants are cut, you will have to clear and reset your tables. In general, it is necessary to be aware of and to adapt to the changing needs of the working environment.

A Waiter's Companion

9 Things to Remember:

- During service, your main function is to be the liaison between your guests and the kitchen.

- The responsibilities of a waiter fall primarily into three areas of equal importance: caring for guests, caring for the restaurant itself, and side work.

- Before your shift, know the soup of the day, the specials, and the 86'd items in the kitchen and bar.

- Write your orders down.

- Provide good service to all customers, even if they are not in your section.

- During service, your primary relationship is with your customer. Maintaining a good relationship with the BOH is a means to that end.

- Be of service to your coworkers in the FOH.

- Guests who feel well cared for will return in the future.

- Strive to provide consistent service for all guests.

Chapter 3: What a Manager Expects from You

A front of the house manager can be thought of as the caretaker of the restaurant. It is her job to look after the best interests of the business and constantly make decisions towards that end. You have been hired, and therefore, it is her hope that you will become a valued asset of the restaurant. Now that you have filled the position, holding on to it will be contingent upon your willingness to learn, your personality and your ability. If your choices and work performance work against the better interests of the restaurant, then it stands to reason that you could lose your job. Two questions that hiring managers typically assess are: "Does this person want to be here?" and "Do they care?"

A manager expects you to arrive for your shift on time. Five minutes early is best so you can be prepared to begin work on time. Issues of tardiness are a reflection of time management challenges. For some, this is a chronic issue and will not be tolerated by your boss for long before you lose your job. This is a basic requirement for all jobs and an indication of one's level of responsibility. It is understandable when circumstances beyond your control complicate your ability to get to work on time. When this happens, be sure to call and inform your boss. This is a courtesy that relieves your manager of the stress of wondering whether or not you are going to show up. But, it is always better to be on time because it is much easier on you to work a shift without the stigma and burden of being the late arriver.

As I mentioned before, a server's primary responsibility is to accurately communicate the guest's interests to the kitchen. There is, however, a large portion of the job that does not involve customer care. Think of yourself as a housekeeper during this time. A restaurant has needs much like a house does; there is always something to clean, fix, fold, or find.

In virtually every restaurant, cleanliness is a major focus. Ideally, a customer should never see evidence of the diner who was there before them. As previously mentioned, crumbs on the table or chair, grease on the saltshaker, lip marks on a glass, or a piece of rice in the fork prong all reflect poorly on the restaurant. I've often heard complaints from coworkers that they are not happy to do this part of the job because they are getting paid less than minimum wage. It's necessary to remind them that the opportunity to generate big money during service includes the responsibility of caring for the restaurant before and after the customers are there.

The attitude you bring to the job is an important aspect of the value you hold as an employee:

As you will find out, waiting can be a very money-focused job. This stems from the way in which we make our money—tips. Each table we wait on makes a decision at the end of a dining experience what to pay us. In the United

States, 15% to 20% for average performance and, hopefully, more for excellent service.

(This point is intended for servers that are paid a tipped wage and who rely on gratuities from guests. It is acknowledged that there are differences in other countries with regard to gratuities and that this point may not be applicable to your work place.)

Assets:

- Willingness to learn
- Pleasant attitude
- Continuously looking for the next chore
- Continues to work while talking to coworkers and regulars
- Has a whatever-it-takes attitude
- Moves efficiently through the restaurant
- Continues to develop product knowledge

Liabilities:

- A know-it-all attitude
- Unwillingness to follow direction
- Unpleasant attitude towards coworkers and/or guests
- Clumsiness, breaking things
- Laziness
- Doing just enough to get by

Unlike other jobs where payment comes hourly or by salary, we are much more aware of what we are making throughout the shift. This money-focused perspective is not an ideal way to move through your shift. I discourage this perspective. It may take some effort to move away from this, but it should have a favorable effect on your working morale. Be realistic with your expectations. There are many different types of people you will serve, from those on a fixed income, to the majority of people in between, to the extravagant diners we call "foodies" who order four courses, a big bottle of wine, and tip twenty-five percent on all of it.

Regardless of whom you wait on, your manager expects a consistency of service across all types of diners. So often, a server will pay more attention to the table spending lots of money and less attention to lower-ticket tables. Aside from the necessary attention a more expensive table requires, the effort must be made to care for lower-ticket tables just the same. Today's table of one could be tomorrow's table of ten. And a complaint from a guest who spent a small amount of money carries just as much weight with your manager as a complaint from a guest who spends big money. Consistency of service is what will bring a guest back through the door, and I assure you, that is the goal of your boss and your boss's boss. Successful restaurants have repeat customers, or regulars. If you make yourself a part of this dynamic, your value, as an employee, will undoubtedly increase.

In closing the money talk, strive to focus on improving your hospitality skills and less on the money. The money will come. I have learned, also, that it is most advantageous to gauge your success on a weekly basis and not each day. Low money shifts will happen, just like big money shifts will, and it averages out in the end.

While you are clocked in, a manager expects you to stay busy. There is usually a running side work list if you are uncertain of what to do. Running side-work is distinguished from opening side-work, which is done to prepare for service, and closing side-work, which is done at the end of service. Running side work is the necessary maintenance, during service, to maintain readiness.

Strive to learn to move as efficiently as possible throughout the restaurant. Use the catch phrase "full hands in, full hands out" to remind you to accomplish this. If you are taking dirty dishes to the dish room, bring clean dishes back out. When you bring a glass of wine to a guest, remove an unnecessary item from the table. If you empty a water pitcher, fill it up: "If you kill it, fill it."

These are examples of habits that will, not only be of benefit when you are very busy, but will also improve the overall quality and efficiency of your job performance.

There exists among most managers and owners an understanding of the journey from inexperience to experience. Learn how to ask for help when you need it. Know that your bosses hold you in a higher regard when you understand your limitations. We all want to generate as much money as we can during a shift, but if the quality of your service begins to suffer because you have taken on more responsibility than you can handle, you will be working against the better interests of the restaurant. If you are asked to take a table outside of your section, make sure you will be capable of caring for all of your guests before saying yes.

Often, employees are guarded when it comes to revealing shortcomings or gaps in knowledge to coworkers and bosses. It seems that this is rooted in a belief that they should know more than they do. This is a perilous approach to the job and is a disservice to your restaurant and yourself. There is no shame in assuming the role of the learner if that is where you truly are. Any manager will be more impressed with an employee who demonstrates accurate self-awareness and the desire to learn, instead of one who hides the true nature of their capabilities. An employee who is willing to learn is a valuable asset and can be worked with and trained, but an employee who poses as someone they are not will inevitably create problems in the working environment. A manager needs to become familiar with the varying skill levels of her employees. With this knowledge, she can staff the restaurant accordingly.

The success of the restaurant depends greatly on the teamwork of the staff. Good waiters always offer assistance to their coworkers when they have a free minute. This help most always comes back around to you when you are in need yourself. When the pressure of the job takes effect, it becomes very easy to slip into a self-centered mentality. It is at these times when you must make a conscious effort to understand the pressures other coworkers are feeling. You may find yourself waiting for your drinks at the bar, becoming frustrated that they haven't been started yet. The bartender is often caring for his customers, as well as making drinks for the servers. Patience is a virtue at these times (A virtue is a quality you cannot live without). If your drinks aren't ready, then take a lap around the restaurant and complete some other task, instead of standing there waiting for them. The bartender will appreciate it, and it is a more efficient strategy. Striving to understand the different job roles around you will help you maintain a respectful relationship with your coworkers.

Communication is essential part of most professional environments, and, in a restaurant, it is a matter of safety. Kitchen people will announce when they are carrying a knife by saying, "Sharp!" You'll know when a hot pan is coming around the corner because—you guessed it—someone yells, "Hot!" Waiters most often say "corner" and "behind" to identify their position around coworkers. This is also very important while walking through the kitchen. Without these simple words, bad things happen: drinks spill, glasses break, food gets dropped, or people get hurt. Be vocal, and don't be afraid to be conspicuous.

There are many phrases and words that characterize restaurant talk. For example, an item that the kitchen is out of is referred to as an "86'd" item. We call tables: 2-tops or 4-tops. Guests who stay for hours and hours are called campers. You should keep restaurant lexicon between you and your coworkers. Generally, it is poor form to address guests with these words. If a guest says, "I would like to have the lamb, please, prepared medium," a server should not respond with, "I'm so sorry, but the lamb is 86'd." Or, it would not be correct to guide a guest to a table by saying, "Right this way. I have a nice two-top for you by the window." There are many other things that a waiter should not say, which are discussed in more detail in Chapter 5.

Your manager usually has much going on. It's important to have a good understanding of what she expects from you. She conducts herself based on her understanding of what her boss expects from her. Pay attention to a manager when they do waiter chores (e.g., sitting tables, bussing, etc.). This is when you can learn what their standards are.

If you are able, help the management in any way you can, so long as it is not at the expense of your primary responsibilities. If a manager is at the host stand taking a phone call and some guests come in, make the effort to seat the guests instead of making them wait for the phone call to end. Most times, your manager will appreciate it. Once you understand the larger picture of how the restaurant business works, then you can have a clearer idea of where you fit in and how you can become better at your job. Be mindful that your manager's concerns include all the activities in the restaurant, not just what's happening in your section.

While working as a server, it is important to know that it is possible to either unintentionally or intentionally engage in criminal behavior. Serving alcohol to people who are underage is one example. If you fail to card a young person ordering an alcoholic beverage, not only can the police ticket you, but your restaurant could be fined and lose their liquor license for a period. Police agencies often conduct sting operations to enforce compliance. This involves sending underage people into a restaurant to order alcohol. If someone serves them alcohol, undercover police who observe the interaction confront the guilty server and inform the manager or owner. When this happens, it usually costs the restaurant tens of thousands of dollars as a consequence, and the server is usually fired. You can avoid this by carding anyone who looks like they're under thirty when they order an alcoholic drink. Think of it as a personal challenge when a person of questionable age orders a drink. It is as if they are threatening your ability to make your money and shut down your restaurant. As a server, it is your right and your job to protect yourself and your employer by asking to see some identification.

If a guest has had a few drinks, it is important to know just when it becomes illegal to continue serving them. Some people handle their liquor well; others don't. It is also important to note that we don't know what the guest might have drank before their arrival. But, once a guest is visibly intoxicated (e.g., slurring words, poor balance, talking loudly and/or obnoxiously) it becomes just as illegal to continue serving them as it is to serve someone under the legal drinking age.

Another potential law-breaking behavior happens when entering credit card tips at the end of your shift. You must enter amounts accurately. If you enter an amount other than what the guest intended, it constitutes fraud, and this can be an issue. Some guests have messy writing or do math incorrectly. Use your best judgment, and ask for a second opinion from a coworker or manager if you are uncertain.

Finally, it's good to find out how the management would like for you to handle a guest with a medical emergency. We all hope things like this won't happen, but the reality is that they will. So, it's good to ask what to do so you can to provide yourself with a course of action. Also, since you work around people who are eating, it's beneficial to know how to do the Heimlich maneuver. It can be very scary to see someone choking. I've had to do the Heimlich twice. One of those times, it was in the middle of the dinner rush and I was running seven tables. From across the dining room, I saw one of my guests jump from his seat, obviously choking. Without hesitation, I went to him and got into position behind him. Fortunately, his airway was cleared after two compressions. It was a scary experience, but it would have been much scarier if I did not know what to do.

Be astute and learn what your manager expects from you. The preceding information is simply a guide based on my experience. There are certainly other factors not mentioned here that may be important to your manager. Learn what they are and do your best to improve your awareness and improve your job performance. It is my hope that the information I have shared will put you on the right track for success.

Chapter 4: Know your Product

A server's fundamental responsibility is to knowing what food items are available from the kitchen and which beverages are available from the bar. From guest preferences to serious food allergies, the development of your product knowledge is a crucial component to your success. When we begin service, we are working to sell our product and restaurant to the guest. You must put in the work to become well informed so that you may confidently field questions from your guests. When you become capable of conducting yourself in this way, your guests will feel more relaxed and confident in your ability to take good care of them. It is the good feeling a guest experiences in your care that creates a desire in them to return to your restaurant in the future.

Some restaurants offer ingredient lists of menu items for server's reference. Others do not. You may not be required to know every single ingredient in every dish your restaurant offers, but typically, you will be expected to know the main ingredients, noting those that may be more common allergens. The avenue to learning this information will arise from a guest's inquiry and, in turn, you asking the kitchen. Collect and store the information you gather; it will be useful again and again. Share it with your fellow servers. Menu knowledge is an ongoing learning process for all servers. This information is vital to the job. We must be able to field questions from guests as competently as possible. Ask other servers what questions they are most often asked by guests about menu items. This is the way to learn.

In a chef's ideal world, guests order their meals and receive them as the chef has envisioned. The reality is that some guests have allergies and food sensitivities that require modifications. It is our job to learn which components can be removed and those that cannot.

Food knowledge becomes very important when it comes to food allergies and specific preferences. Whether the reason is a medical condition, weight loss goals, social or religious beliefs, or simply an interest in overall wellness, the landscape of dining out has changed, and it is our job to fulfill the guests' desires and field their questions with competence. Remember, the customer chose to dine in your restaurant, so it is important to be patient and provide the appropriate service to demonstrate your respect for the guests' right to know what they are eating and to make choices that are right for them. Be sure always to include any specific allergy information on the ticket to the kitchen. From gluten-free, dairy-free, vegetarian, and vegan, to food allergies to nuts, soy, or shellfish, you must prepare yourself to expect these situations.

Many people are sensitive to spice. Therefore, it is important to make yourself aware of the spice level of various dishes your restaurant offers. As a person who enjoys spicy foods, it has only been through experience that I understand the sensitivities of those whose tolerances are lower than mine. For some, simple black pepper used in food preparation can be too much. Come up with an effective way to characterize spice levels in dishes. This can prevent the guest from not enjoying their meal or the unpleasant experience of having to send a dish back to the kitchen.

Once you have completed your initial training, focus on completely learning a dish or two each shift you work. Learn how to describe it, its size (modest, normal, or large, etc.), the cooking process, and any other important selling points. Think of your words as a brush painting a picture in the guest's mind: "Our salmon this evening is wild and line-caught from the Columbia River–just arrived fresh this afternoon. It's going to be brushed with a citrus vinaigrette, pan-seared, and finished in the oven."

It is also important to describe dishes to guests without expressing your personal opinions, unless solicited. When describing an item I am not particularly fond of, I will often add, "People enjoy that dish." This leaves me open to be truthful if asked my opinion: "It's not one of my personal favorites, but if you are in the mood for seafood, I think the scallops are an excellent choice." You want to avoid dwelling on a negative opinion for long and move on to something positive as quickly as possible.

When it comes to accumulating knowledge of the food you serve, there is no better teacher than firsthand experience. When an opportunity presents itself to taste, do so, and think about how you would tell a guest about it. Note the spice level and any predominant flavors. There will be many opportunities to taste in the kitchen, and as I mentioned before, it is important to ask the chefs before you take food to eat. It is good to continually build your experience and food knowledge to improve your service, but it's extremely disrespectful to take without asking. In most cases, the kitchen staff simply wants you to show the respect of asking. Not doing so is one of the quickest ways to lose the respect of the kitchen.

Like knowledge regarding food, bar knowledge merits a mention, too. When you are new to the beer, wine, and cocktail world, the sheer volume of information can be intimidating. No one expects you to learn it all in a day, a week, or even a month, but learning a little each shift is certainly expected.

Here's a breakdown of important information:

The well liquors are the least expensive, and these are poured unless premium liquor is specified.

Typically, there is a well vodka, gin, tequila, rum, and whiskey/Scotch. Learn what they are.

Premium, or call liquors, are the nicer-quality brands. Learn these, too, so you can upsell.

Guest: "I'd like a Manhattan."

Server: "Do you have a bourbon preference?"

Guest: "What do you have?"

Server: "Our well is Old Forester. We also have Jim Beam, Maker's Mark, Knob Creek, and Basil Hayden's."

A Waiter's Companion

Guest: "I'll have Maker's Mark."

Server: "Would you like that up or on the rocks?"

Guest: "Up."

Many guests will just be interested in well drinks, but when you know the premium liquors your bar offers, you can provide your guests with the option to upgrade. Your ability to upsell adds up over time. You can increase your sales over the course of a shift, and in a week, you may increase your bottom line significantly.

Also, learn secondary questions about cocktail presentation, such as what drinks can be served up or on the rocks. For instance, single malt Scotch can be served on the rocks, neat (not chilled and served without ice), or with water. Martinis can be served up (chilled but served without ice) or on the rocks, and dry or dirty. Learn what these mean. Specialty martinis are usually served up, but find out from your bartender to be sure.

Learn the beers that are on tap as well as those in bottles. Memorize them from lightest to darkest. Learn what lagers, pilsners, ales, porters, and stouts are.

Know what IPA's (India Pale Ale) you carry. Also, find out what N/A (non-alcoholic) beer is available, as well as other available non-alcoholic drinks.

Wine is a vast world that takes years in which to become competent. When starting out, learn which wines are white and which are red:

White
- Chardonnay
- Sauvignon Blanc
- Pinot Grigio
- Riesling

Red:
- Cabernet Sauvignon
- Merlot
- Pinot Noir
- Malbec
- Zinfandel

These are simply a few examples of the more common varietals (grape types). There are many more to learn. House wines are like well liquors—the basic qualitative level. Then there are premium wines, which can be quite expensive. People who drink wine know this and don't mind paying for a quality wine if that is their taste. Guests who simply order a house red or white aren't interested in premium wines. It is never okay to choose a premium wine for a guest who orders a house wine. They will be most displeased when they see on the bill that their "house wine" costs $22 a glass.

As you acquire descriptive wine terms, learn which wines are dry and which are sweeter. Most wines are dry, and when a guest asks for a "sweet" wine other than White Zinfandel (an inexpensive, sweet rose wine), they usually want a wine that is fruity or fruit forward. So, learn to distinguish between a dry wine and a fruity wine. Learn from more experienced waiters around you, and even if your palate is not yet able to distinguish between differing qualities of wine, remember the importance of learning.

As a young server, I did not understand why a guest could be so finicky about selecting a wine. What I have learned is that, as a person's palate becomes more experienced and mature, they become more sensitive to the subtle nuances of flavor. Different grapes produce wines with different characteristics. As you begin to acquire wine tasting experience, learn to distinguish them in regard to body (light, medium, or full), acidity, and fruitiness. A "well-balanced" wine has the proper amount of acid and fruit characteristics.

Another component of service regarding wine is food pairing:

> Guest: "What wine do you recommend if I order the halibut?"
>
> Server: "By the glass or by the bottle?"
>
> Guest: "By the glass."
>
> Server: "The Pascal Jolivet Sancerre would complement that dish nicely."

Without getting into too much detail on the subject, an excellent question to ask when tasting a new wine is what foods it would pair well with. Take notes and remember pairing information for future recommendations to guests.

As you gather experience, you will begin to see patterns regarding which types of wines pair with various foods.

You will eventually become comfortable with everything your restaurant has to offer, but it is a long road. As long as your boss sees that you are putting in the effort to learn, you will be on the right track. Some chefs will give you the "what for" when you ask a question they believe you should know. You may have to take some static, but don't let that stop you from asking. All of this knowledge is paramount and a big part of your job description. Don't let your belief of what you think you should know stop you from acquiring information by asking.

5 Things to Remember

- There is a confidence that comes from knowing your menu.

- Learn which of the more common allergens (i.e., dairy, eggs, fish, shellfish, wheat, soy, peanuts, and tree nuts) are in various dishes.

- Learn how to characterize the spice levels of dishes on the menu.

- Draw a distinction between describing a dish to your guest and sharing your opinion of it.

- Learn beers, wines, and liquors, as well as the secondary questions to ask when guests order cocktails.

Chapter 5: What We Say and What We Do

This is a business of little details. A guest's pleasurable experience is the result of a server's management of a hundred little choices. That's why an attentive manager will scrutinize your actions. It's important that you make the effort to learn the way your restaurant wants things done. Some tasks may be handled in a variety of ways, whereas others may require a specific course of action. Common sense does not always mean common practice. Therefore, this is the chapter of details. Once the previous guiding principles take hold and your appearance is on point, what you say and what you do becomes the next focus. The guiding principle this chapter presents is striving to avoid awkward interactions and vague communications with guests. It is our responsibility to pay attention to the quality of our interactions. This chapter contains examples of optimum word choices, and suggestions on technique, to streamline the quality of your service.

A guest's dining experience begins the moment they walk into your restaurant. Their experience becomes your responsibility as soon as the hostess leads them to your section. From this perspective, I would like to invite you to consider the importance of what follows.

When a guest is seated at a table that has an organized and clean appearance, it sends a message that their dining experience is beginning appropriately and is being handled professionally. When a guest is seated at a table that has not been sufficiently cared for after the previous party and lacks careful organization, it sends a message to the guest that they have been seated in a section in which the server is not capable or does not care about providing competent service. Mind you, the customer realizes all of this before you even greet them personally. Therefore, it stands to reason that, to provide professional service, you must learn to value organization, precision, and cleanliness within your section. By doing so, you communicate to your customers that you care about yourself and your service, and you ensure them that you will provide a pleasant dining experience. Once again, your guests realize all of this before you approach the table.

To recap, your responsibility for the guest's dining experience begins when they are seated in your section, not when you greet them. By the time you approach the table, they have already begun to think, "This is nice," or "Yikes, fairly unkempt. I'm concerned."

Reflecting upon the aspects of a truly professional and successful waiter, it is imperative to understand how human nature evolves as people mature. It is a great challenge for less experienced people to understand what matters to those farther down the road of life. There is the reckoning of presence, word choice, and the principled nature you bring to your guests. In theory, it may seem like a bigger issue than it has to be, but it creates all the difference between simple service and professional service. As people mature, the words and demeanor you share with them take on greater value. Word choice may be outweighed by how you share those words (i.e., inflection and tone.) Learn what this means, for it is important, and it will help you connect with your guest.

Over the years, a person tends to fine-tune how they speak to people, generally discarding what is awkward and keeping more successful terms and phrases. That middle-aged gentleman who handles himself with sophistication and grace certainly did not always behave that way. It is an ongoing process to get to the point where verbal interaction becomes an artistic and pleasant experience.

In hospitality, there is a professional boundary between you and your guest that you should assume from the start. A common mistake many servers make is becoming too casual too quickly with guests, either verbally and/or physically. What one person considers a friendly pat on the back, another may construe as an invasion of personal space. Some people simply do not like to be touched by a stranger, no matter how positive the intention may be. As hospitality professionals, we should assume this boundary until a guest makes it clear that they are open to a more personal interaction.

An experience comes back to me involving a man with whom I worked a few years back. Upon my arrival at work one day, I greeted him with a pat on the back, something I had done many times before. This time, he turned around and said, "Do you have any idea how rude that is?" I was speechless, not understanding his hostility. We certainly were not strangers, but we weren't close acquaintances either. When I shared the incident with my manager, he said to me that in my coworker's culture, it was considered rude to touch a person you are not familiar with. This had never occurred to me; I considered myself a friendly, backslapping, nice guy. My manager continued. "In some cultures, people shake hands as a greeting. In others, people bow to each other. Think about it." That was my lesson, which, of course, carried over into how I've learned to treat guests. If a customer chooses to demonstrate a relaxed boundary with you and, say, extends his hand to shake yours or gives a friendly touch, then the guest is showing that it is okay to be more casual. Let the guest set the tone. Assume a professional distance otherwise.

With regard to speaking, don't share too much personal information with a guest unless they prompt you to do so. Some guests like to ask questions to get to know you while others do not. It is fine to answer their questions, but only if the guest initiates the conversation and your time talking is not at the expense of your other tables. It is also important skill to learn how to appropriately break rapport without being awkward. The vast majority of guests understand that you have things to do, but there is always that one guest who is oblivious to the rest of the world. It's important to know how to break rapport. If you are not able to resolve the conversation verbally, you can use your body language to communicate that you must leave the table. If that doesn't work, you can excuse yourself to do a walk around your section by saying, "Let me make a round, and I'll be right back."

Furthermore, if a customer introduces himself, be sure to remember his name. Write it down when you take his order, and use it as often as possible. People love to hear their name, so if a guest offers it, say it as often as you can. Not to mention, this action demonstrates your attentiveness.

Once you feel comfortable with the primary guiding principles that put you in the mindset to provide competent service, there are many smaller, yet important, components in a waiter's toolbox. Here are some of the more specialized tools to put you squarely in the professional realm. Strive to provide excellent service instead of settling for giving average service.

The way we speak can play a significant role in the tone we, as servers, set at a table. It is important to present yourself to the guest in a comfortable and competent manner. If you approach a table of two men and two women and say, "How are you guys doing?" this could be considered rude since the table is mixed company, not all guys. Nowadays, we seem to hear this word choice everywhere. But this is a casual way of addressing people and has no place in a professional exchange. I'm certain this is a generational preference. Older people generally do not prefer to be addressed as 'you guys.' Demonstrate your awareness of this by, instead, saying,

"How are you all doing today?" or simply, "Hello! Welcome."

Also, consider what you might say when you inquire whether a guest is done eating.

Some say, "Are you still working on that?" There are better ways to make this kind of inquiry.

People do not go out to eat to "work." Eating out is a pleasurable experience, not work. Instead, one can say, "May I clear?" Or, a simple hand gesture towards the dish may be enough. You can also ask, "Are you still nibbling, or may I clear?" These small details are not small, because, as a server, you set a tone at your table with the words you choose. That is why I am taking the time to impress upon you its importance.

There is a distinction between the way you talk with your friends in a casual setting and the way you speak while working. When speaking to guests, say "yes," not "yeah" or "uh-huh." Also, say "you're welcome," "of course," or "my pleasure" instead of "no problem." The vast majority of the professional waiters I have worked with have eliminated this latter phrase from their table dialogue. It is a response that has come to replace "you're welcome" in our culture. "No problem" is a phrase uttered every day countless times. It seems to have become so mainstream that it is almost universally accepted as an appropriate response to "thank you."

"No problem" is comprised of two negative words put together to construe a positive sentiment. However, I have seen time and again that people, especially mature people, can be put-off by hearing it. As I mentioned before, there is an art to social interaction, thus maintaining a pleasant experience for all. This tends to become more important as people grow older, and sometimes all it takes to diminish a dining experience, and the quality of your rapport, is choosing the wrong thing to say. These suggestions will help you become more professional, and if you are a young person waiting on a table of mature people, I assure you, something this simple will impress.

A pleasant dining experience is the accumulation of a hundred small details that all come together. It's mostly about what you have done, but also about what you didn't do—interrupt, hover, rush, or make your guests wait for you. Being a good waiter means instilling confidence in your customer that you know what you're doing. This sets them at ease.

We all have varying types of voices. Some naturally fill a room, while others are barely heard. Voice projection certainly merits discussion here. If your voice is naturally soft, then it behooves you to practice speaking at a volume in which you can be heard by your guests. When you are at a table, it is important to speak as clearly as possible and at an appropriate volume. Older people, who may not hear as well as those that are younger, can become frustrated if they do not understand what you are saying to them. If you happen to notice a guest who, through body language, communicates that they are having trouble hearing you, reposition yourself closer to them. Likewise, if you notice a guest with hearing aids, adjust your voice and/or position accordingly.

As we reviewed in Chapter 2, when checking back with a guest to ensure that they are satisfied with their main course, your word choice is important. We call this the "two bites or two minutes" check back. This gives your guests the opportunity to inform you of anything with which they may be dissatisfied. Through my experience, it became evident that it is better to ask questions that can be answered with a "yes" or "no" response from the guest. This approach eliminates the possibility of an awkward interaction. "Are you enjoying your meals?" or "everything tasting good?" may be answered with a simple yes or a nod if they have a mouthful of food. Avoid asking, "How is your meal?"

Super-quick service isn't always the best kind of service. Strive to move as efficiently as possible, but be aware that your guests may feel the urgency of your actions, and it may also be apparent on your face. Make an effort to approach your guests with a calm and controlled demeanor, even if you are feeling rushed. You want to create a comfortable environment where guests can feel relaxed and enjoy themselves. To this end, it is also important to be aware of your facial expressions. At times, when we are busy and caught up in the moment, our faces may reveal our worry. Guests will notice this and feel your haste. Train yourself to maintain an even, controlled look no matter what you may be feeling underneath.

As you approach a table with food or drink, be sure to approach in such a way that the guest knows you are there. People talk with their hands, and a gesture can spill a glass of wine or topple a plate of food. Don't surprise a guest by approaching from behind. Let your presence announce itself. The art of engagement includes eye contact, which is so important. Make your guest feel cared for. Make an effort to make eye contact when you deliver food and when you leave the table.

Before serving appetizers, clear an area on the table before they arrive. This prevents the guests from scrambling to do it themselves when the food arrives. Also, when you pick up food from the kitchen, think about the orientation of your guests. Hold the plates so that you may serve your guests without awkwardness.

Remember, you run your tables. Don't let your tables run you. Learn to be forthcoming with your guests about your intentions when you leave and what information you would like to collect when you return. After greeting your guests and telling them about the specials, you may say, "I'll return shortly to see what else you'd like to drink." Or, as you are delivering drinks, you may say, "Do you have any questions about dinner, or shall I return in a few minutes?" Developing this type of serving style gives structure to the exchange and allows you to run the table instead of your guests running you. It is also important to learn how to avoid getting trapped by an indecisive guest. Guests don't always understand the pressures of your job, nor should we expect them to. It is our job to learn how to manage our time. A major part of this skill involves graciously breaking away from a table that would prefer you to stand there while they discuss the merits of the chicken saltimbocca and the veal Milanese amongst themselves. Unless you are actively involved in the decision-making process, feel free to say, "Take your time. I'll come back in a few minutes," or "There's no need to rush. I'll be back by in a few minutes."

Also, it bears repeating that you should be efficient in your visits to the table. Every time you bring something to a table, take something away. You should remove items that guests are no longer using, like empty wine glasses, appetizer plates, empty sugar packets, etc. When doing so, take note of any silverware that you need to replace. While providing table maintenance, you may ask, "Is there anything I can offer at the moment?" or "Do you have everything you need?"

When clearing cocktails or spirits on the rocks, unless the guest places their glass in a position that makes it obvious they are done, always ask, "May I take this?" before doing so. An example is a single malt Scotch on the rocks. This drink is consumed to the last drop. As a matter of fact, some people will consume all the ice. So, be careful about being too presumptuous when the drinks appear to be finished.

A Waiter's Companion

When clearing plates from a table, there is an order in which you should proceed. Let's consider a 4-top, two men and two ladies. In scenario one, both men and one woman have finished their meals, while the other woman, who has been doing most of the storytelling during the evening, is still eating. Each of the three who are finished has placed their forks and knives neatly together on their plate, waiting for the woman to finish her meal. This presentation indicates that you, as their server, shall wait until all meals are finished before you clear. In scenario two, we have the same table and same guests, but instead, the woman who has finished her meal has stacked her bread plate on her dinner plate. One of the men has shoved his plate to the side and has placed his napkin on it. In this scenario, these actions indicate that you should clear those two positions immediately.

There are people who prefer to keep their empty plates in front of them until everyone at the table has finished their meal. The idea behind this practice is that it is considered impolite to rush anyone who may eat at a slower pace, and to leave one person with their food while you clear the rest of the table does just that. Experienced diners know this and will not stack or shove plates until everyone at the table has finished their meal.

To recap, there are three situations in which a server may clear while others are still eating:

- When plates are shoved to the side
- When plates are stacked
- When napkins are placed on top of entrée plates

Otherwise, it is polite service to clear all plates when everyone has finished.

The restaurant landscape will always have children present. We must make every effort to prevent issues and keep a keen awareness of our professional space. Never pass food, clear items, or serve plates over babies in carriers. Parents are very protective of their babies. It would be a huge mistake to spill or drop anything on them. Make an obvious effort to demonstrate that you are aware of the baby, and take care to avoid such an incident. It is also important to be aware that you may need to hasten your service for diners with children. They may want the pace of their dining experience to move along faster than leisurely diners. Often, parents have a limited window of opportunity in which to enjoy themselves when children are present. You can avoid a full-on meltdown by stepping up the pace when waiting on families with little ones. Read your guests to determine if this is necessary.

It's tacky to drop the check before everyone has finished eating unless your guests request it. When that time comes, there are some things for you to consider when putting the bill on the table. Often, your guests may continue their conversation long after you have dropped the bill. Depending on how you have put the bill on the table will dictate how things unfold. There are times when your manager needs you to turn a table for the next guest. So, it's important to consider what follows:

Don't set the checkbook up on end partially opened. The reason I suggest this is that you eliminate your recourse for action if your guests do not address the bill promptly. Instead, place it flat on the table. When you do this instead, you create the option to approach and look in the book to see if your guests have offered payment. This action also reminds your guests that the bill is on the table. If payment is not in the book, you can simply say, "No rush. I just wanted to make sure you weren't waiting on me." Consider putting the book on the table in an orientation that faces you instead of the guest. This way, you will know by looking at the book if the guest has opened it and looked at the bill. Some people place their credit card inside the book and close it. Therefore, it can be unclear if they have even looked at the bill. But if the book is facing the guest, you will know that they have looked at it. This is a helpful practice that gives you more awareness regarding guests who don't employ effective nonverbal communication regarding payment time.

Finer Points:

- When a guest doesn't have their reading glasses while reading the menu, be sure to write the bill amount in large print at the top of the receipt.
- Carry reading glasses with you for your guests who forget theirs.
- Carry a small flashlight in case you have to look under the table for an earring backing or something else that has dropped.

When a guest pays with cash and there is change to be made, make it easy for them to leave a proper tip by returning change in appropriate bills. Never say, "Do you need change?" This is a tacky and presumptuous question. Instead, when picking up the payment book, say, "I'll be right back with your change." A guest is always more than happy to tell you, "It's all yours," or "No change."

Before returning to the guest with credit card slips to sign, take a moment to ensure the pen you are providing to the guest is working. It is inconvenient for the guest when he is prepared to leave but must flag you down for a working pen. This could be avoided by simply creating a habit of ensuring that you are providing a working pen.

Finally, when guests get up to leave, look the table over for things like phones, glasses, baby items, or food packed to go that the guest may have forgotten. It is also important to make sure the guest has not left their credit card behind. Quite often, a guest will inadvertently take the signed copy of the credit card slip. When this happens, the server may lose out on the tip.

Therefore, it is perfectly acceptable to collect the checkbook from the table before they leave. This can be done discreetly, perhaps while refilling a beverage, or, if it feels necessary to say something, put your hand on the book and ask, "Is this all set?" If this feels uncomfortable to you, it won't once you lose out on your money a time or two. Sometimes, despite your vigilance, guests will leave before you can check for the signed copy. I have found it effective to place the credit card slips on top of one another as opposed to placing the customer copy in one pocket and the restaurant copy in the other. The reason for this is that often, if the guest takes the signed copy, the imprint may be decipherable on the bottom copy. Be sure to check with your manager that this is okay, but usually, as long as the guest's intention is verifiable, you will be able to collect the tip.

The way we conduct ourselves in the restaurant merits some discussion. Go out of your way to give the guest the right-of-way when walking through the restaurant. If you accidentally bump into a chair occupied by a guest, be sure to always acknowledge it. Never ignore it and walk away. A discreet "pardon me" or "excuse me" is all it takes.

If it is necessary to point across the dining room while talking with a coworker, develop the habit of pointing with an open hand instead of pointing with a finger. This is simply a more professional way of handling yourself while directing a coworker's attention in the dining room. When you point with your finger, a guest may feel as if you are pointing at them.

Another mistake so often made by both FOH and BOH employees is discussion of an employee's health within earshot of guests. We all get colds, and as long as we are vigilant of how we handle ourselves (e.g., coughing into the crease of our elbow and refraining from touching our face and eyes), one can successfully complete a shift while minimizing the spread of germs. But, when a guest hears any of the staff speaking about how much cold medicine one of the cooks has taken, it may cause concern and should thus be avoided. Also, make an effort to avoid restaurant chatter within earshot of guests. They are not interested in overhearing your gripes about your work schedule or issues about another table.

As a tipped employee in the front of the house, it is in poor taste to discuss the money you make within earshot of any back of the house employees. Most BOH employees are not interested in hearing about the amount of money waiters make. Their hourly wages are lower, and it creates animosity.

Put things back where they belong so the next person who needs something will be able to find it. This is a fundamentally important practice that we all should have learned from our parents. The development of this simple habit not only ensures that the next person needing that item will find it, but it also maintains a sense of order in what can easily become a disorganized and chaotic workspace. It also behooves you to clean up after yourself if you make a mess in the server station, but remember: The easiest mess to clean is the one you don't make in the first place. Strive to work with precision and keep work areas clean.

During service, guests like to see servers engaged in productive activities. Your downtime should be spent cleaning and doing side work like polishing silverware and folding napkins. Activities like giving other staff member massages or standing around chitchatting reflect poorly on you, look unprofessional to guests, and will garner negative attention from your manager. Make the effort to be constantly productive.

You will learn many new words in the restaurant business. Food items and names of wine can present a pronunciation challenge to those new to the business, and even to those who are not. Quinoa, jicama, foie gras, aioli, crudité, and charcuterie are some examples. Wines, especially French and Italian wines, also require some pronunciation practice. If you are uncertain, be sure to ask someone who knows. Avoid mispronouncing words to a guest.

Each restaurant is a whole different world. Learn how things are done in yours. What is considered correct in one restaurant may be incorrect in another. Restaurants strive to provide good food and consistent, competent service. Do your part to strive for this within yourself as well.

8 Things to Remember:

- Strive to avoid awkward interactions and/or vague communications with guests.
- A guest's dining experience begins before you approach and greet the table.
- There is a professional boundary that exists between you and your guest.
- The way we speak plays a significant role in the tone we, as servers, set at a table.

- Make an effort to approach your guests with a calm and controlled demeanor, even if you are feeling rushed.
- You run your tables. Don't let your tables run you.
- Be efficient in your visits to the table. Every time you bring something to a table, take something away.
- Put things back where they belong so the next person who needs it will be able to find it.

Chapter 6: Nonverbal Communication

Body language is an important component of communication. It demands that we take time to study and strive to understand how people employ it and how to react to it appropriately. As you expand your job awareness, your ability to notice and react to nonverbal communication from your guests will enable you to provide a more seamless dining experience. Furthermore, learning to observe the guest's unspoken gestures elevates the quality of your service. This chapter will help to increase your understanding of the importance of becoming a keen observer in your work environment of those, often overlooked efforts of your guests, to communicate with you.

It's impossible not to communicate, even when you are not saying a word. How you stand, together with the fleeting micro-expressions of your face, conveys important information about you. It can show that you are nervous and uncertain as well as if you are calm and confident. "Incongruence" occurs when your verbal messages are at odds with nonverbal messages, and this creates tension. Strive to have your words and your body language in alignment with each other. If you behave in a relaxed confident manner, the person you're talking to will likely feel relaxed too. We all possess empathetic mirror neuron circuitry, in which we reflect the body language of those who we are talking to. For some it comes naturally to communicate with ease. For others, it is a skill to develop. What follows is a collection of suggestions that, if assimilated and employed, will undoubtedly improve your service as well as your self-presentation.

Often, when guests first arrive and are seated, they may be engaged in conversation. Your initial approach and greeting may appropriately be more discreet than normal. Although it is necessary to greet them promptly so they know who their server will be, pay attention to their actions and adjust your service accordingly. It is customary to allow your guests to get settled before offering appetizers and drinks, other than water. This is, of course, if your diners are leisurely. If your guests present as knowing what they want immediately or are in a rush, then adjust your service accordingly. Once the guests begin to read the menu, it is the right time to approach and mention specials, daily soup, etc.

Attentiveness is an important component of proper service. Even when your tables appear to have everything they need, be sure to make yourself visible to your guests every few minutes. You can do this by walking through your section, making unobtrusive eye contact as you walk by. This practice gives your guests the opportunity to get your attention if they need something. Even if they have everything they need, guests will feel attended and not forgotten. As a server, it is easy to get distracted by conversation in the kitchen or elsewhere. While these things happen, train yourself to remain aware of your tables, no matter where you are in the restaurant or what you may be doing. Do not be out of sight from your section for too long a period of time.

While most nonverbal communication occurs between you and your guests, there are some basic behaviors between you and your coworkers that can be considered to fall into this category. For instance, while walking through the restaurant, make the effort to pass others left shoulder to left shoulder as often as possible. Think about walking through the hallways of school. There are unmarked lanes of travel that naturally occur that result in a semblance of order in a potentially chaotic situation. It's the same in a restaurant. This basic sense of order is core to smooth operations when the restaurant is busy and can reduce the possibility of collisions.

It is also important to learn how to act respectfully towards your coworkers. An example of this involves the situation where the server is waiting at the window for a line cook to complete a dish that is to be served. As they are putting the final touches on a dish, it's inappropriate to wait with your hand open in the window, waiting to receive the dish. This action could be viewed as insignificant, but it is not. The cook will place the dish in the window when it is ready. That is your cue to take it. We must learn to wait without creating a sense of rushing our coworkers. Most experienced workers move with a sense of urgency, both in the front and the back of the house. Although you may feel compelled to hurry the process along by displaying your sense of urgency to complete your order, it is in poor form to display this haste to the cook in the window.

There are many different types of guests that you will wait on. Some are more experienced communicators than others. Although it is our job to adjust our service to the style most appropriate for the guests, there are those who have mastered the art of nonverbal communication. They know how to use their eyes and their posture to let you know that they would like your attention. Often, they may be involved in conversation but will discreetly gesture with their eyes or a tilt of their head to let an attentive server know they are ready to order. It is important that you make yourself visible to your guests every few minutes. This means that you make eye contact with each of your guests as you walk through your section. This practice also provides you with the opportunity to scan each table for beverage refills or any dishes ready to be cleared. Ideally, no more than ten minutes should pass between such check-ins.

There is an entire art to dining on the part of the server, as well as the diner. Some guests are highly experienced at communicating their needs to a perceptive server without saying a word. It can truly be a pleasure to wait on these people because the experience usually unfolds very smoothly, provided that you are tuned in to the situation. Subtle body movements and facial expressions are sometimes all that are necessary for an experienced diner to let you know they are ready to order or have their table cleared. Make an effort to observe these gestures, and you will be sure to make your customer feel at ease and cared for. When this type of guest sees that you are tuned in to this level of awareness and communication, they will certainly reflect it in their tip to you.

When the dining experience is winding down, be sure to look for a wallet or credit card on the table, indicating your guest is ready for the bill. It is typical for people to "fight" over who will pay the bill. The rule to follow is that whoever gives you the credit card first is the one who pays. Savvy guests will excuse themselves from the table and give their credit card to you when you are away from the table. If this occurs and another guest hands you their credit card later, you can simply say, "it's already been taken care of."

It's important to honor the one who was first to give you their card.

When you have collected the credit card to run the payment, do your best to make the wait as short as possible for the guest. This is when the guest is going to decide what to pay you, so remain aware, and don't make them wait any longer than they have to.

And finally, know that we humans are hardwired to have opinions and judge others within seconds of encountering them. Is this person friend or foe? First impressions count, and I cannot overemphasize the value of a smile. Most people pick up on a fake smile. It involves the muscles around the mouth, but not the eyes. A real, heartfelt smile involves the muscles around the eyes as well as the mouth. The biggest and best difference you can make in regards to approachability lies in the power of a genuine smile.

4 Things to Remember:

- Body language is an important part of communication.
- Learn how to read guests' body language.
- Become aware of how your body language affects those around you.
- There is tremendous power in a genuine smile.

Chapter 7:
The Hygiene Boundary

Our behavior is determined by our beliefs, and our beliefs generally arise from our awareness. Our awareness expands when we keep ourselves open to learn from other, more experienced, people. This chapter is intended to expand your awareness about the hygiene boundary that exists between you and your guest. This is an extremely important behavioral concept for a professional server to understand. The hygiene boundary is defined as a server's awareness, and resulting behavior, that respectfully acknowledges and prevents the transfer of germs from one guest to another, and from himself to the guest.

People who are sensitive to this boundary will always notice when a server violates it, as well as when it is appropriately respected. They will rarely, however, verbally acknowledge either, and simply take note of it. Employees who behave in a manner that demonstrates their cluelessness of the hygiene boundary present as poorly trained and are a reflection of the standard of the ownership and management of a restaurant. The consistency of an environment where workers are taught to respect the hygiene boundary will do more to ensure repeat business than an environment where germ transfer does not appear to be a priority of the restaurant. It is of paramount importance to understand the facets of this boundary and shift your behavior accordingly.

The server who respects the hygiene boundary demonstrates thorough and professional training, and an ever-growing awareness of the hospitality mentality.

The way you present yourself is important. Personal hygiene requires attention and awareness. A professional appearance begins with a clean uniform over a bathed body. We become nose blind to our body scent/odor. Therefore, it is important to remain aware of this fact and tend to our cleanliness every shift. You should not emit body odor, and, on the other side of the spectrum, you shouldn't wear heavy cologne or perfumes. Perfumes, lightly applied, are okay, but amounts that are overwhelming can be as distracting, to your guest, as a stinky uniform. Strive for a neutral, non-offensive middle ground.

Hairstyles must not require constant maintenance with your hands. Although your hair may be fresh and clean, it is considered unsanitary to touch your hair and scalp while handling items touched by guests. Choose a hairstyle that is pulled back and out of the face, and train yourself not to self-groom in view of guests. This will reflect your awareness of the hygiene boundary, both to your guests, and to your managers alike.

Before we explore other intricacies of the hygiene boundary, it is necessary to discuss the idea of germ transfer. As we mature, our life experience teaches us how germs are transferred from one person to another. Some guests are acutely aware of this while others are not. It is the responsibility of the restaurant staff to strive to conduct themselves in a manner that demonstrates an understanding of germ transfer and the effort to prevent it.

The fundamental idea of the hygiene boundary itself is to keep the interior surface of your hands sanitary. This is the part of your hands that touch everything from a guest's glass to their plate of food, to the bill you bring at the end of the meal. This is why it is important to teach yourself to use the back of your hand to itch your face and any other type of personal maintenance. When you cough or sneeze, do it into the crease of your elbow or shoulder instead of your hand. If you need to scratch your nose, use the back of your hand and wrist, not your fingers. Perception is reality for your guests. If you reach up to scratch your nose with your fingers in a customer's line of sight, it may appear as if you are picking your nose. When attempting to separate two napkins or pages that are sticking together, don't wet your fingers with your tongue to do so.

Guests are more comfortable when they feel the environment they are dining in is clean and sanitary. One can evaluate a restaurant's cleanliness by observing employee behavior and the dining room's appearance. Therefore, it is important and necessary to learn the difference between appropriate and inappropriate behaviors and techniques.

When bringing articles to the guest and servicing the table, your awareness of the hygiene boundary must be evident in your actions.

Although you may be successful at keeping the inside of your palms sanitary, it is still important not to touch items that have been or will be in a guest's mouth. When handling items like silverware and straws, be sure not to touch these parts (i.e. the prongs of the fork and either end of the straw). Handle all silverware, whether clean or used, by the handles and not the parts that touch food. Don't bare-hand clean silverware in the dining room. If a customer requests a spoon or fork, either use a marking tray to bring it to them or hold the utensil in your hand on a cloth napkin. Unless straws are in a wrapping, deliver them to the guest in a beverage napkin (bevnap). When handling beverage glasses, don't place your hands on the rim of the glass where the guest places their mouth to drink. When you refill water or deliver drinks, be sure to pick up and hold the glass low, away from the rim. It is never okay to serve a glass with the palm of your hand above the top of the glass and your fingers around the rim. This is a blatant violation of the hygiene boundary.

This idea also applies to the proper way to handle used glasses when bussing a table. To be efficient when one does not have a tray, some people will pick up dirty glasses by clenching them together with their fingers down inside them. Although this technique is very common, it is an extremely unsanitary practice. A person's mouth germs are on the rim of the glass that is now in contact with the employee's hand. Germs are then transferred to whatever they subsequently touch. A guest may see this and wonder whether that employee handled items on their table. It is simply an unsanitary technique that demonstrates a lack of awareness and professionalism.

When refilling beverages, don't clank or rest the vessel on the rim of the glass while pouring. Simply allow the liquid transfer without contact. Also, when refilling a glass with a straw in it, don't allow the straw to contact the pitcher while pouring. Sound silly to you? Perhaps. Although it may not matter to you, guests notice details, and for some, such cluelessness chips away at your professionalism and your tip.

When clearing a table without a tray, pick up only what you can comfortably and properly carry. The key point here is that it is important to act with awareness in your direct dealings with the guest, as well as the indirect dealings that they observe. In restaurants that utilize pepper mills, one should not place it high under their arm. Armpits sweat, and we certainly wouldn't stick our hands in our armpits any more than we would touch something that's been there. Instead, grasp the pepper mill against your body, as close to the elbow as possible, while holding salads in your hands.

When guests leave the table, some waiters will fold a guest's cloth napkin. This practice is a nice touch as long as the napkin isn't over handled. Remember, the guest has been using it to wipe their mouth. It can be picked up by the corners and tri-folded for neat table placement without touching it excessively.

When wiping a table, start with the table itself, and then wipe seats. If you clean chairs before tables, the place where a guest's backside was for an hour and a half has now been wiped across the eating surface, or at least that is how it may be perceived. Therefore, the order is important. When wiping down multiple tables, wipe all tables first, then the seats. This is a simple practice that demonstrates your awareness.

The preceding information is by no means an extensive or complete list of all the details of the hygiene boundary. It is, however, an introduction to the concept and is intended to be a foundation to build upon. Recent world events have elevated our collective awareness of germ transfer and it is more relevant now than ever to learn to conduct ourselves with these ideas in mind.

4 Things to Remember:
- When guests see the service staff employ proper hygienic techniques, their appreciation increases, and they may be more likely to return in the future.
- A server should constantly maintain a clean and professional appearance.
- Refrain from placing your hands on surfaces that a guest's mouth touches, such as the rim of a glass, the tip of a straw, or the parts of silverware that touch food.
- Use a tray when bussing a table, or carry no more than you can appropriately and comfortably handle.

Chapter 8: Things That Can Go Wrong

Yes, things will go wrong. No matter how much you pay attention to your tables and your responsibilities, sometimes powers beyond your control can send a dining experience into a tailspin. The vast majority of situations, however, can be prevented once your awareness increases. Developing a course of action is key to the proper resolution of most challenges.

When the phone rings at the restaurant, it is customary to answer it within three rings. If you take a call, it is imperative that you relay and/or record any pertinent information. Until you pass the information to the proper personnel or write the information down in the proper place, it is your responsibility, simply put. It is extremely unprofessional and quite embarrassing when a guest arrives with a party of eight, saying that they have a reservation when it is not written in the book. If it is possible to scramble to accommodate them, it is a fortunate save. If a reservation is not relayed to the book on a busy night, it may be impossible to accommodate them. One can avoid all of this by simply following through and ensuring that a reservation is recorded on the proper day and at the correct time.

At the table, things can go wrong, too. Upon your initial approach, be sure to identify gender before you greet guests. I once greeted a table of four, saying, "Good evening, ladies," only to realize that one of the long-haired people was a man. Not only was it embarrassing for him and me, but it also immediately demonstrated my lack of attentiveness—not a good start.

Guests also very often have their cell phones on the table with them. Take care not to spill beverages on them. When refilling drinks on patio tables with wired surfaces, take care not to miss the glass, as the beverage can go through the table onto the guest's legs. In restaurants that use tablecloths, often two or more tables are pushed together to create a larger table. Ideally, we strive to level the tables so they are seamless and even with each other. Realistically, it is sometimes impossible to get the tables to line up correctly. I have seen spilled glasses of wine and iced teas because the guests set them there, unaware of the ridge underneath the tablecloth. If this is the case, you can discreetly point it out to the guest to avoid a spill.

Guests often request items during their meal, like more dressing for their salad, cream for coffee, or a drink refill. These requests may be easily forgotten when you are busy. Although it may be a small detail to you, realize that your guest's continued enjoyment is dependent upon your delivery of that item. Ensure that your guests have the necessary silverware for each course, such as a spoon to stir their coffee. Be sure to follow through on these little details. It makes all the difference.

A Waiter's Companion

A waiter who forgets is failing at a fundamental level of the job. Even if you are young and your memory is sharp, without developing thorough habits, you will forget. We are, by definition, multitaskers. When you write down orders, it frees you up to do the next thing without having to hold on to the information in your head. Sometimes, you may encounter three or four other tasks before you are able to put the order in the computer. If you do forget a particular detail about an order, it is a far better decision to return to the guest and confirm the information instead of running the risk of getting it wrong when meals are delivered. By that time, the flow of the dining experience is disrupted while you and the kitchen remedy the salmon dish that requested sauce on the side. Train yourself not to forget your guest's information.

When you do encounter an unhappy guest, it is a priority to remedy the situation promptly. It's important to learn how your boss would like for you to handle an unhappy guest. This is something you want to discover as soon as you begin your training. The following scenario includes a resolution that has proven successful:

A guest calls their server to the table shortly after entrées are delivered. He tells her his steak is cold and overcooked. She immediately removes the plate and apologizes one time, then offers to have another out to him as soon as possible. He proceeds to tell her he is interested in something else. "Would you care to see a menu?" she offers.

He says, "No, I'd like the prime rib instead." At this point, time is of the essence because the others have food in front of them, and he doesn't. First, she goes to the kitchen to fire the entrée, and then she informs her manager of the issue. In some restaurants, the manager may handle communication with the kitchen. However, the goal is to expedite the return of an entrée to the guest as soon as possible. Once it arrives, she thanks him for his patience and asks if there is anything else he needs. She checks back within two bites or two minutes to ensure he is happy.

Here are some key points to remember:

- Remove the offensive item from the table immediately. One of the biggest mistakes a server can make is to leave an unwanted item in front of the guest. She will not eat it, and she will continue to grow more discontented the longer she stares at it.
- Apologize once. Profuse apologies are unprofessional and befuddled guests may continue to dwell unnecessarily on the issue. It is an interesting quality of human nature, but when a person apologizes profusely, it sometimes causes the guest to complain continually. One apology is sufficient. Then move the situation along towards a resolution.
- It is also in poor taste to share excuses with the guest when things go wrong. There are certain situations where it may be appropriate to give a reason why an issue occurred, but the general rule is to keep excuses from your customers. It is most often appropriate to simply acknowledge a guest's frustration by saying,

A Waiter's Companion

"Thank you for your patience," or "Sorry to keep you waiting."

Once there has been an issue at a table, it is very important to ensure that no more occur, not so much as an empty water glass. After an issue occurs, diners tend to scrutinize the rest of the dining experience. A dinner with a mistake can still be a great dining experience, as long as you handle the mistake promptly and properly and provide competent guest service for the remainder of the meal.

The degree to which a dining experience falls short depends a great deal on your customer. Some are very understanding, whereas others become irate. One time, as I stood at the bar waiting for the bartender to pour some glasses of wine, a gentleman from my 8-top of businessmen walked up behind me and tapped me on my shoulder. I turned to see him holding his half-eaten salad plate up at eye level. Without saying a word, he directed my attention to a little green worm inching its way around the edge of the plate. Fortunately, this man was very understanding once the manager explained that our greens arrived at the restaurant prewashed, and that little worm went unnoticed. The manager expressed our embarrassment as well, and that was all he could do. Fortunately, this gentleman was not put off nor did he become upset. But imagine for a moment if that worm was found in the salad of a squeamish woman who could have been extremely offended by this experience? It could have been much worse.

As bad as that was, this next story characterizes my worst experience. I was working in an Italian restaurant on a busy Friday night. One of my tables consisted of an elderly couple, their adult son, his wife, and their five-year-old daughter. I was getting a refill of Sprite for the little girl when I went to the oven to get warm garlic bread for another table. I set the Sprite down, turned to get the bread out of the hot oven, picked up what I thought was my Sprite, and delivered it to the little girl. About a minute later, the father of the girl stood up and yelled across the restaurant, "You served my daughter alcohol!"

I went straight over, apologized, and took the drink to the bartender. Meanwhile, this man was fuming, red faced and irate. The bartender smelled the drink, stuck a straw in, capped the top of it with her finger, and pulled it out to taste it. She determined that it was straight tonic water, no booze. (Whew!) I went back over to inform the man that there was no alcohol in the drink, but he cut me off and said, "I quit drinking five years ago, but I still know what alcohol tastes like. Wipe that smirk off your face. Why, I should take you outside and do it myself."

At this point, there was no changing this man's mind. He convinced himself that the situation was as he believed it to be. I had to walk away at that point because he was red-faced, with veins popping out of his neck. Just about that time, my coworker, Jeremy, came up to me and said, "I served a man at my table a Sprite instead of tonic water." It turns out that Jeremy also went to the oven at the same time I did. He set his tonic water on the counter and got his bread.

He then turned and picked up my Sprite and sped off. Unbeknownst to me, I took the tonic water to the girl at my table. And that was all it took to ruin the dining experience, not only for that particular table, but also for the others who witnessed his nasty behavior. There is a certain quality to tonic water that can be mistaken for alcohol, and this man, who was a dry alcoholic, was inconsolable, convinced his daughter had taken a sip of alcohol. The important thing to remember is to get your manager involved as soon as possible. It is their job to handle these types of situations, and it is a healthy practice to keep your manager informed of any situation that has the potential to become an issue. Communication is the key.

Substandard cleaning of dishes can be common in some restaurants. Sometimes, entrée dishes are stacked clean, for kitchen use, with food stuck in between. Unfortunately, this sometimes happens due to oversight in the dishroom. When preparing to serve entrées to a table, take a moment to feel the underside of the plate for old food. If your restaurants have white tablecloths, this is especially important. It is more than unbecoming when you clear a finished meal from a guest's position, and there's a stain left behind, from old food from another guest, in front of them. Prior to bringing a stack of appetizer plates to a table, inspect each plate to ensure they're clean before bringing them to your guests. This is an excellent habit to develop and demonstrates your attention to detail.

When it comes to payment time, and the guest gives you a credit card, it is of utmost importance that you handle it with care while away from the guest. There was a coworker of mine who had lost track of a credit card before running payment. He had the whole staff looking for it. After about fifteen minutes (which is far too long for a guest to be waiting) it was discovered under the POS (point of sales) computer. He never figured out how the card ended up where it did, but he could have avoided the whole situation by employing a fail-proof system. Often, a credit card is collected in the payment book and placed in the little pocket at the top of the check presenter where it can be seen. I have found it most effective to put the card in my breast pocket while I place the payment book in my apron. This prevents the possibility of the card getting knocked from the book while in the apron. It is also acceptable to relocate the card to the checkbook pocket inside instead of leaving it sticking out where it can be knocked off and dropped. Either way, the idea is to secure the card so you cannot lose it. Other times, the guest hands you their card before you bring their check. I make sure they see me place it in my breast pocket. Also, when running multiple payments for one check, have a system in place to prevent yourself from running two payments on one card. Developing successful habits to prevent issues is the main takeaway.

If a guest flags you down because their server has not greeted them, don't make them continue to wait for service while you track down their server. Get a drink order and inform them that you will send their server right over. Be sure to give the drink order to their server or inform them if you have already submitted the order. The idea is to provide service as soon as possible. These people have already been waiting awhile if they are moved to ask for service. This is also an example of why it behooves you to make an effort to be aware of which coworkers are in each section. It reduces the time you spend looking for the server.

When it comes to certain issues with improperly cooked items, consider the best ways to handle the situation. For example, if the fish is undercooked on a salmon salad entree, it may be best to slide the fish onto a side plate while leaving the entrée salad in front of the guest. This way, the guest has something in front of them to eat while you attend to getting it properly cooked. In other situations, a proper solution could be offering a cup of soup while an entrée is corrected. Generally, you want to avoid leaving a guest with nothing in front of them while the others at the table have entrees. Ask your manager how they would like you to handle such situations.

The development of proper techniques can prevent many situations from escalating into more serious issues. However, if an issue arises, be prepared with a course of action that will resolve it as quickly and appropriately as possible. Successful issue resolution can often save a dining experience from crashing and burning.

Most often, it is the little details that, if not addressed, lead to bigger issues. When a guest becomes agitated because his beverage has not been refilled in a timely manner, he begins to scrutinize every little thing that is not going well. One of the basic indications of suitable service is keeping water glasses full. It is one of those things that people notice, much like the cleanliness of the bathrooms. It is an indication of how the business is run. So, when a guest becomes agitated, it becomes more difficult to provide a pleasant dining experience.

My father is an iced tea drinker. If his glass sits empty for too long, he gets frustrated, and it becomes difficult to enjoy our experience. He can throw back five or six glasses in a sitting. So, take note if you have a thirsty guest at your table and ensure drinks stay filled.

As you accumulate more experience, your ability to handle more responsibility will expand and grow. Learn how to manage yourself and when to say no to additional responsibility that's offered if you are unable to maintain the level of service the guests deserve and expect. A great dining experience for your guest is the result of a hundred little decisions you make over a couple of hours. Learn from your experience and become a little better every shift you work.

Conclusion

In hospitality, as in life, the best teacher is experience itself. In order to grow, you must remain open and pay attention to the lessons as they come your way. It is my hope that the insights and suggestions I've shared will provide a framework that you can fill with your own experiences that are most relevant to your environment. We want to strive for the qualities that are held in high regard at the fine dining level, even if most restaurants are not fine dining establishments. Therefore, I'd like to leave you with the concept of serving at a level of refined dining. This idea is based on the pursuit of providing proper service, despite the qualitative level of a restaurant. Refined dining simply means that your service quality meets and exceeds the hospitality standard that is in place amongst the dining public. Great service leaves a guest with a good feeling about a restaurant, and that good feeling brings them back in again and again. This is what you should strive for, no matter your restaurant level. A key factor in this pursuit is coming to understand how values change as people mature. As a person ages, their life experience becomes more nuanced in the details of interaction with people. Your influence on others is the most valuable currency there is. The confidence you develop through your experience provides you with the ability to create more meaningful interactions with your guests. People appreciate sincerity, and when your customers like you, they'll reflect that in your gratuity.

You will create a memorable dining experience when you tend to a hundred little details resulting from your knowledge, word selection, table presence, attentiveness, and timing. Be there when you are needed, but don't be intrusive. Be attentive, but don't hover. Adjust your type of service based on your perception of your customer's needs. Don't lose sight of what's happening—a professional service interaction for your restaurant. It's not a time to make friends, nor is it a time to share information that's too personal, unless it is appropriate to loosen the professional standard of conversation for regulars, or it's made clear by the guest that it's okay to do so.

Ultimately, restaurants should be a fun and social environment where people share good cheer. Eating out should be an enjoyable experience for the guest, and a restaurant should be a comfortable environment for you. It is our job, as servers, to keep our stress tucked away behind our expressions so we don't take away from the guests' ability to enjoy themselves. The unfolding of your hospitality mentality will certainly contribute to the success of your restaurant, and also to your own personal sense of satisfaction and accomplishment. Cultivate the best version of yourself and strive for improvement every day.

"If you love life, then don't waste time, because time is what life is made of.

–Bruce Lee

About the Author

Jon Bee has worked in hospitality since the mid-1990's. He has worked in a wide variety of restaurants, spanning the spectrum from casual buffet style to distinguished DiRoNA and Four Diamond award-winning, fine dining establishments.

Jon realized a need in the hospitability industry for a comprehensive resource for those waiting tables.

His experience, coupled with his desire for continual professional improvement, led to the creation of A Waiter's Companion. Jon hopes that this book will not only elevate the quality of service for all who enjoy eating out, but also provide a tool for managers and restaurant owners to utilize towards that end. Jon lives in Boulder, Colorado.

Notes

You may use these following pages for personal notes.

A Waiter's Companion

NOTES

A Waiter's Companion

Notes

A Waiter's Companion

NOTES

A Waiter's Companion

Notes

www.ingramcontent.com/pod-product-compliance
Lightning Source LLC
LaVergne TN
LVHW050024080526
838202LV00069B/6908